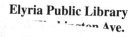
Kristi Yamaguchi

by Elaine A. Kule

Raintree

Chicago, Illinois

Printed and bound in China by South China Printing Company.
10 09 08 07 06
10 9 8 7 6 5 4 3 2 1

Library of Congress Cataloging-in-Publication Data:
Kule, Elaine A.
  Kristi Yamaguchi / Elaine A. Kule.
      p. cm. -- (Asian-American biographies)
  Includes bibliographical references and index.
  ISBN 1-4109-1057-1 (hc) -- ISBN 1-4109-1130-6 (pb)
  1. Yamaguchi, Kristi--Juvenile literature. 2. Skaters--United
States--Biography--Juvenile literature. 3. Women skaters--United
States--Biography--Juvenile literature. I. Title. II. Series.
  GV850.Y36K85 2005
  796.91'2'092--dc22

                              2005005637

Acknowledgments
The publisher would like to thank the following for permission to reproduce photographs:
AP pp. 18 (Wide World Photos), 25 (Wide World Photos/Laurent Rebours);
Corbis pp. 4 (Frank Trapper), 13 (Bettmann), 22 (Neal Preston), 31 (Sygma/The Oregonian), 32 (WallyMcNamee),
50 (Frank Trapper), 56 (Reuters/Kimimasa Mayama); Courtesy Kristi Yamaguchi pp. 8 (Always Dream Foundation),
11 (Always Dream Foundation), 54 (Always Dream Foundation), 58 (Always Dream Foundation); Getty Images pp. 7
(Time Life Pictures/Eliot Elisofan), 14 (Hulton Archive), 20 (Todd Warshaw), 27 (Doug Pensinger), 29 (Shaun
Botterill), 34 (Agence France-Presse), 36 (Agence France-Presse), 38 (Agence France-Presse), 43 (Liaison/Bill
Greenblatt), 45, 46 (Time Life Pictures), 48 (Allsport/Ian Tomlinson); Sports Illustrated p. 40 (Heinz Kluetmeier);
Superstock p. 46 (age fotostock); World Figure Skating Museum and Hall of Fame p. 53 (Galon Wampler).

Cover photograph: Corbis (Frank Trapper)

Special thanks to Kristi Yamaguchi's Always Dream Foundation and Carole Yamaguchi for their help in the
preparation of this book.

Every effort has been made to contact copyright holders of any material reproduced in this book. Any omissions will
be rectified in subsequent printings if notice is given to the publisher

Some words are shown in bold, **like this**. You can find out what
they mean by looking in the glossary.

Contents

Kristi Yamaguchi is a role model for millions of people. She devotes her time to family, friends, fundraising, and planning and performing in skating events.

Introduction

Kristi Yamaguchi [yah-ma-goo-chee] is one of the world's greatest figure skating champions. During her career she won 22 titles as a singles and **pairs** skater. Among her awards is an Olympic gold medal she earned in 1992. It was a dream come true for Kristi, who had practiced for hundreds of hours, learning and polishing the difficult movements. Her freestyle program for the event showed the graceful dancing talent that brought pride to her family, her country, and her many fans.

Kristi was born in the United States, but she has always been proud of her Asian heritage. Kristi's mother's grandparents and her father's parents left their homes in Japan in the early 1900s. They settled in California and tried to fit into their new community. They dressed like their American neighbors, gave their children American names, and spoke only English at home.

World War II

But during World War II, their lives changed. On December 7, 1941, Japanese soldiers bombed a naval base in Pearl Harbor, Hawaii. It brought the United States into the fight against Germany, Italy, and Japan. It also brought distrust and anger toward Japanese-Americans. These loyal U.S. citizens were considered enemies and faced widespread **discrimination**. The U.S. government forced them to leave their homes and live in **internment camps**, officially called relocation centers. The camps were surrounded by wire and watched by soldiers.

Kristi's father, Jim, spent part of his childhood in a relocation center in Arizona. Her mother, Carole, was born in a camp in Colorado. Despite the discrimination he faced, Kristi's grandfather was a U.S. Army officer in Europe.

Jim and Carole met in college. Although they weren't taught Japanese growing up, they shared a pride in their Asian and American backgrounds. Kristi's parents taught her Asian customs and American traditions. She learned Japanese folkdances and wore a **kimono** on special occasions. The Yamaguchis also exchanged gifts at Christmas, wore costumes for Halloween, and watched fireworks on the Fourth of July. Kristi's awareness and appreciation for both cultures always stayed with her.

During World War II, the U.S. government built relocation centers, or internment camps, and forced Japanese-Americans to live in them.

Kristi started figure skating when she was very young.

Chapter 1:
Childhood Dreams

Kristi Tsuya Yamaguchi was born on July 12, 1971, in Hayward, California, a city near San Francisco. She is the second of three children of Carole Doi Yamaguchi, a medical secretary, and Jim Yamaguchi, a dentist. Kristi's sister, Lori, is two years older. Her brother Brett is three years younger.

When Kristi was a baby, her parents saw that her feet turned in and curled under. To correct the problem, she wore leg casts and foot braces until she was two years old. Walking in the casts was difficult for Kristi. She wobbled at first, until she learned how to balance herself.

When Kristi was four, her mother took her to dance classes to strengthen her feet. Lori was already enrolled. Kristi adored her big sister, so she was happy to join her. By then the family was living in Fremont, California, a city near San Jose.

A New Discovery

The girls also took baton-twirling classes and performed in a local parade, Kristi's first public performance. Years later Lori became an award-winning twirler, but by age four, Kristi put away her baton. She discovered figure skating and it changed her life.

Kristi saw her first ice show while shopping in a local mall with her mother. Watching the skaters twirl around the ice in pretty costumes fascinated Kristi. She wanted to skate, too. But her mother thought she was too young. As Kristi wrote in her **autobiography**, *Always Dream*:

"We saw more ice shows, and I kept begging to skate.
'When you start school and can read, then we'll see,' Mom promised.
I came home from my first day in first grade and announced:
'I can read! Now can I go skating?'
Mom kept her promise."

Figure Skating

Historians believe that ice skating began in Europe in 50 B.C.E. For hundreds of years, people strapped animal bones to the leather soles they wore on their feet. Ice skating started as a form of transportation in cold places, like Scandinavia. It became a sport in England in 1100 C.E.

Kristi tried many things as a young girl, including baton-twirling and cheerleading, but nothing gave her as much enjoyment as figure skating.

Figure skating—a combination of ice skating and dance—began in the United States in 1864. Until then, skating had been a stiff and routine sport. Jackson Haines, an American ballet dancer, changed all that when he appeared in ice shows featuring the big leaps and fast spins he created. Many Americans disliked his performances and thought the sport should stay as it was. Haines traveled to Europe, where his new style on ice was well received among audiences. After figure skating became an Olympic event in 1908, it gained acceptance in the United States.

Learning To Skate

Kristi and her mother went skating with a friend and her child. Kristi could barely stand in the rented skates, so her mother held her under the arms while skating behind her. Kristi laughed as they circled around the rink. She had so much fun, and she wasn't at all afraid of the ice.

Kristi thought the skates were hers, so when it was time to leave, she wouldn't give them back. She soon understood what renting meant. Whenever she and her mother returned to the rink, Kristi requested and wore the same skates.

Kristi's hopes and dreams grew as she did. Her new goal was to skate in an ice show. She liked entertaining. She and her friends often wore costumes and put on little shows for their families and neighbors. Although she was shy about speaking in class, Kristi enjoyed performing for people.

In 1976 the **media** was excited about figure skater Dorothy Hamill winning the Olympic gold medal. Kristi had seen Hamill's beautiful skating and hoped to be just like her. Months later she received a Dorothy Hamill doll. Kristi loved it so much she took it to practice with her every day.

Dorothy Hamill

American figure skater
Dorothy Stuart Hamill was
born on July 26, 1956, in
Chicago, Illinois. She
began skating when she
was eight years old. While
a teenager she won many
important championships,
including the Ladies'
Figure Skating gold medal
in 1976 at the Olympics in
Innsbruck, Austria.

Hamill's great talent, attractiveness, and sweet nature made her an
international star. She created a skating spin called the "Hamill
Camel" and toured for years with a show called the Ice Capades.

The first modern Olympic Games were held in Athens in 1896.

The Olympic Games

The Olympic Games are worldwide athletic contests held in a different city every four years. They are considered the most important international sporting event. Only the best athletes from each country are allowed to participate.

The Olympic Games started in ancient Greece in 776 B.C.E. In 393 C.E. Emperor Theodosius ended the games. The games were restarted as an international event in 1896 with an aim to encourage peace, friendship, and athletic competition among countries.

In 1924 the Olympics were divided into the Summer Games and the Winter Games. In 1994 the International Olympic Committee decided to hold the Summer and Winter Games every four years, two years apart from each other. The Winter Games last for about two weeks and holds over 78 contests, including the ice skating events. Athletes from approximately 75 countries compete for gold, silver, and bronze medals.

A Shy Student

Kristi's mother enrolled her in group ice skating classes. In the beginning Kristi cried from shyness before each session. Once the lessons began though, Kristi focused on the skating and her tears stopped.

When Kristi was six years old, she worked with her own coach, Ann Cofer. They met twice a week. Kristi and her mother woke up early for two hours of practice skating before the school day began. Cofer had Kristi keep a log, or journal, of each session, writing down every jump and spin she did.

When Kristi was seven, she entered her first skating competition–and won. But to Kristi, skating wasn't about prizes or outdoing other children. She skated because she loved it and wanted to perform well. Kristi worked hard, and won more local championships.

A New Coach

At age nine Kristi attended a summer camp for skaters. She met Christy Kjarsgaard, [yars-guard] a skating coach well known in the northern California area. Kjarsgaard heard about Kristi's ability and wanted to work with her. Soon Kjarsgaard became Kristi's coach.

The change was difficult for Kristi and her mother. They had to wake up at 4:00 a.m. every morning to meet Kjarsgaard at the rink by 5 a.m. After Kristi skated for five hours, her mother drove her to school.

To keep up with that schedule, Kristi went to sleep when it was still daylight. But she loved her sport and wanted to become even better at it. Kjarsgaard taught her many of the difficult jumps, spins, and turns competitive figure skaters need to learn.

Kristi was nine years old when she first met Christy Kjarsgaard.

Christy Kjarsgaard

Christy Kjarsgaard started figure skating when she was four years old. She skated in competitions throughout her childhood and reached the U.S. National Championships. While attending the University of California at Berkeley, Kjarsgaard began teaching other figure skaters. She graduated from college in 1974 and made coaching her full-time career. Since 1976 Kjarsgaard has coached at least one skater at the U.S. or Canadian National Championships almost every year.

In 1995 Kjarsgaard moved to Lafayette, California, where she is Figure Skating Director at the Oakland Ice Center.

Hard Work and New Challenges

Kjarsgaard thought her young student should also enter **pairs** competitions. At age eleven Kristi was matched with a local skater named Rudy Galindo. Rudy was a strong, talented skater, but he had many difficulties facing him. His family was very poor and his mother was mentally ill. Skating helped him forget his troubles.

In addition to her morning skating, Kristi practiced with Rudy for an hour after school with their pairs coach, Jim Hulick. Kristi's parents were proud of her ability and accomplishments, but they insisted she keep up with her school work. Because Kristi was a good student, her junior high school principal let her have a part-time schedule. She did her homework and studied hard for tests.

For seven years, Rudy Galindo and Kristi skated together in pairs contests all over the world.

Dreams Come True

Kristi and Rudy skated together in various figure skating contests. Kristi spent so much time with Rudy that she considered him a brother as well as a skating partner. Rudy even lived with the Yamaguchis for awhile. The family's steady home life was good for him, and it was a shorter distance to and from practice sessions.

Kristi and Rudy went all over the world together and met skaters from many nationalities. Wherever she visited Kristi noticed the strong bond among skaters. Differences in language, culture, and nationality were unimportant. They all loved their sport, and they understood one another.

In 1987 Kristi won the World Junior Skating Championship in the Junior singles category. She and Rudy also captured the **pairs** gold medal. After many hours of hard work and sacrifice, Kristi's dreams were coming true.

This photo shows Kristi with her mother. Kristi has always been close to her family, and their support helped her in tough times.

Chapter 2:
On Her Own

I n high school Kristi faced a problem. The school in her neighborhood only allowed full-time enrollment. At first, Kristi worked with tutors, but she knew she was missing out on an important part of her life. She wanted to be around other teenagers. For the eleventh and twelfth grades, she attended Mission San Jose High in Fremont, California.

A Special Present

Kristi enjoyed school and did her best to fit in while balancing her skating and academic responsibilities. During her final year at school, she and Rudy won the 1989 U.S. National **pairs** title. Kristi also took second place in the U.S. ladies singles event. She became the first woman to win two medals in the Nationals contest in 35 years. To honor that achievement, the students at Mission San Jose gave Kristi a letter jacket worn only by the school's best athletes.

Kristi had good friends at school, but she was looking forward to graduating. She knew she had to train full-time to become the best figure skater she could. But there was a problem. A few months before, Kjarsgaard, Kristi's coach, married and moved to Edmonton, Canada.

Moving Away

Kristi liked training with Kjarsgaard, who had become a friend. She did not want another coach. Kjarsgaard invited Kristi to live with her. Kristi agreed, but it was a hard choice to make. Kristi had always been close to her family. Saying goodbye to everyone was difficult. But, one day after graduating from high school, Kristi moved to Edmonton.

Kristi and Rudy had practice sessions when they could meet in Canada or California. But the many miles between them hurt their partnership. They were also upset by the death of Jim Hulick, their **pairs** coach, who died at 38.

Tragedy Strikes

Only five days later, Kristi's grandfather, George Doi, died. Kristi took the loss hard. Her grandfather had attended many of Kristi's skating appearances. He cheered her victories and comforted her disappointments. Now he was gone. She cried for days, knowing she'd never see him in the stands again or at family gatherings. The heartbreak was the worst Kristi had ever known. She couldn't even think about skating.

Kristi and Rudy won the U.S. Nationals pairs title in 1989 and 1990.

But she knew her grandfather and Jim believed in her talent and would have wanted her to pursue her goals. Kristi and Rudy won the U.S. Nationals pairs title again in 1990, a fitting **tribute** to their coach.

Encouragement

Kristi came in second in the singles category. She was very angry with herself. Still she had the 1990 World Championships to look forward to. Kristi and Rudy spent hours on their routine. The friendships Kristi formed with many of the other skaters helped support her. Before Kristi's performance at the World championships, skater Tai Babilonia gave Kristi a heart-shaped earring along with a friendly note. The act meant a lot to Kristi, and she wore the earring for many contests.

A Difficult Break

Kristi and Rudy came in fifth place at the championships. Kristi placed fourth in singles. It was a big disappointment. For the first time, Kristi gave serious thought to quitting competitive figure skating. Instead Kristi decided to quit pairs skating.

Kristi's break with Rudy was difficult. For seven years, they had been a team, practicing together and depending on one another. Kristi knew she became a stronger skater by working with Rudy. But now she was on her own.

These skaters took first, second, and third places in Ice Dancing Free Dance at the World Figure Skating Championships in 2003.

World Figure Skating Championships

The World Figure Skating Championships is an important contest organized by the International Skating Union (ISU). The ISU consists of countries from around the world. It was founded in Europe in 1892, and is the oldest international winter sport **federation**. The group's purpose is to establish rules for skating competitions.

The first World Figure Skating Championships held outside Europe for men, women, and **pairs** competitions took place in New York City in 1930. The first ISU meeting held in Asia was in Kyoto, Japan in 2002. In 2003 the World Figure Skating Championships were held in Washington, D.C., the event's first visit to the U.S. capital. Skaters from 40 countries competed.

The Canadian skater Kurt Browning helped Kristi to improve her skating. He remains a good friend.

Chapter 3:
Winning the Gold

Now that Kristi could put her thoughts and energy into one effort, singles skating, she worked harder than ever. But at the 1991 U.S. Nationals, Kristi came in second for the third year in a row.

Kristi knew her performance was weak. The winner, Tonya Harding, put on an amazing show by landing all of her **triple jumps**, including the first **triple axel** by an American woman.

For weeks after that event, Kristi felt miserable. She put so much time and effort into preparation for the Nationals and still fell short of her goal. Then Kurt Browning, a Canadian skater who won four world championships, told Kristi to let her love for skating show, even during practice. He also said she should smile sometimes!

Browning's advice changed Kristi completely. The joy of skating was back, and with good results. Four weeks later Kristi won a gold medal at the 1991 Ladies Singles World Championships.

In January 1992 Kristi's thoughts were on the Olympics. But she only hoped to perform well at the historic event. As Kristi wrote in her autobiography, *Always Dream*:

"This might be hard to believe, but no one in my family, or Coach Christy, ever talked about me winning the gold medal. In fact I wouldn't allow myself to think about it…I thought that would jinx me. I remember paging through a magazine before the Games and coming across a big picture of the medals. I instantly slammed the magazine shut without looking."

At the 1992 U.S. Nationals, where she had felt so defeated the year before, Kristi performed beautifully and received a gold medal.

New Challenges

Many people believed Midori Ito of Japan had the best chance of winning the gold at the 1992 Winter Olympics in France. After all Ito had performed the **triple axel** even before Tonya Harding.

Despite hours of trying, Kristi hadn't mastered the challenging jump. Every day Kristi tried spinning in the air three-and-one-half

In 1991, Tonya Harding became the first American woman to land a triple axel jump.

times and landing firmly on one foot. Each time she either fell or lost her balance.

Learning the other triple jumps—the **Salchow**, the **Lutz**, the **toe-loop**, **loop**, and **flip**—was easy for Kristi. But the triple axel seemed beyond her reach, and it would not be in her Olympic program. Many people thought that omitting the triple axel would hurt Kristi's chances of winning a medal.

The Lutz

The **Lutz** was first performed as a single jump in 1913 by Austrian figure skater Alois Lutz. The jump requires using the right toe pick to lift the skater off the left leg. The Lutz uses the left outside edge of one skate to make one full rotation in the air and land on the back outer edge of the other skate.

The Lutz is special because it is the only jump in which the skater begins the jump moving in one direction and finishes the jump skating the opposite way.

The Spirit of The Games

Kristi tried to ignore the pressure that came with the Olympic Games. She decided to participate in them as they were meant to be played, with feelings of goodwill and peace.

The figure skating competition would start eleven days after the Games began, but Kristi enjoyed that time. She walked in the opening ceremony, feeling thrilled and honored to be part of a grand tradition. During that time Kristi met Bret Hedican, a hockey player for the U.S. team, who became important to her years later. She had fun living in the Olympic Village with athletes from around the world, and watched several sporting events.

Kristi took part in the opening ceremony at the 1992 Winter Olympics.

This picture shows Kristi performing at the 1992 Winter Olympics.

Kristi's practice sessions were going well. Soon the day arrived for figure skating's **short program**. But as Kristi stepped onto the ice, a wave of self-doubt swept over her.

Kristi remembered the note she received from her **choreographer**, Sandra Bezic: "This is your moment, let it shine."

Kristi gave a terrific performance. It helped her confidence, because when she had to compete again two days later, she wasn't as nervous. She was one of six finalists, and she was glad she made it that far.

Waiting backstage to begin her **long program**, Kristi was surprised when her childhood idol, Dorothy Hamill, came up to her and wished her good luck. Encouraged by Dorothy's words, Kristi glided onto the ice. She skated well, until she slipped while landing a **triple jump**. To keep her balance, Kristi's hand touched the ice.

Mistakes

Kristi was horrified, but she thought quickly. For the first time ever, she changed her program in the middle of a performance, choosing a double **Salchow** instead of a triple, which had given her trouble before. Toward the end of her performance, she kept the triple **Lutz**. Kristi always felt comfortable with that jump; in fact, she had learned it in just one day. Still, anything could happen, and she couldn't make another error.

Kristi leaped into the air and landed solidly to thunderous applause. Relieved she smiled at the audience and skated off the ice. Overall she was pleased with her performance. Another skater could take first place, but Kristi knew she did well for herself and for the United States.

Kristi watched the other five finalists. They also made mistakes. Two of the women, Tonya Harding and Midori Ito, fell during their triple axel jumps. Kristi Yamaguchi had won the gold medal.

A New Life

When Kristi learned she won the gold medal, she could hardly believe it. She was the first U.S. gold medalist in ladies figure skating since Dorothy Hamill in 1976. Stunned, she climbed to the top step of a podium and stooped as the gold medal was placed around her neck. Hearing Francis Scott Key's "Star Spangled Banner" was an experience Kristi would always remember.

Doing the very best she could at a sport she loved was a dream come true for Kristi. She had come a long way from the little four-year-old watching her first ice show. She was an Olympic champion, a gold medal winner, a world-famous figure skater. She was 20 years old, and her life would never be the same.

Midori Ito

Midori Ito was born on August 13, 1969 in Nagoya, Japan. She started competitive ice skating when she was six years old.

Over time Midori became known for her skillful jumps, thrilling audiences with the athletic ease of her performances. At the 1989 World Figure Skating Championships in Paris, she became the first woman to land a **triple axel** in a major international contest. She also became the first Asian skater to win the Championships.

After winning the silver medal at the 1992 Winter Olympics, Midori skated professionally, placing first in several competitions. In 1993, at the World Professional Championships, she became the first woman to perform a triple axel in a professional competition. At the 1998 Winter Olympics in Nagano, Japan, Midori was the first torchbearer and lit the Olympic Cauldron in the opening ceremonies—a great honor.

After years of hard work and dedication, Kristi won an Olympic gold medal and fulfilled her dream.

An American Dream

Many large companies ask Olympic champions to **endorse**, or promote, their products. Two weeks after the Olympics, Yamaguchi signed a contract to endorse clothes made by a fiber company. Other endorsements followed.

One month later Yamaguchi captured the World Championships in Oakland, California, near her hometown of Fremont. It was an especially meaningful win for that reason, and a happy way to end the 1992 figure skating season.

By then there was great **media** interest surrounding Yamaguchi. Everyone wanted to meet her, including other famous people. She was interviewed on television shows. Her photograph appeared on magazine covers. *Sports Illustrated* magazine featured Yamaguchi on the cover with the heading, "American Dream."

Articles were written about her. Invitations poured in for Yamaguchi to attend events across the nation. She had more fans than ever.

Kristi was pictured on the cover of Sports Illustrated magazine in 1992.

Chapter 4:
A Star on Ice

In 1993 Yamaguchi achieved another longtime goal when she signed a contract to skate with the Stars on Ice tour. She would perform for people all over the world and skate with the sport's biggest stars. Her days as an **amateur** were over.

Yamaguchi looked forward to becoming a professional skater. She thought it would be easier than the hard work she experienced most of her life. The Stars on Ice organization and the athletes were friendly and helpful. She found a good friend in Scott Hamilton, a fellow Olympic gold medalist whom she had known since childhood. Yamaguchi also grew close to pairs skaters Sergei Grinkov and his wife, Ekaterina Gordeeva.

But going from an ordered lifestyle to one of traveling five or six months a year was a big change for Yamaguchi. The Stars on Ice show was two hours long. It toured about 70 U.S. cities and several countries each year. The training was as hard as before, and Yamaguchi was often homesick.

But Yamaguchi loved performing. There was still that magic, the bright lights and costumes that always appealed to her. She liked experimenting with music and dance steps. And she enjoyed the appreciative crowds. The show was, after all, about entertaining people and making them feel a part of the program.

Family and Friends

Yamaguchi's definition of family broadened over the years. She formed close bonds with the cast, crew, and organizers of the Stars on Ice show. While touring they spent a lot of time together, and grew to care for one another.

One morning in 1995 Sergei Grinkov seemed his usual happy and healthy self. Later, while practicing with his wife, Ekaterina, Sergei suddenly collapsed on the ice. Shortly afterward he died of a heart attack. He was only twenty-eight years old.

It was a terrible shock for the group, especially for his wife and their three-year-old daughter. Yamaguchi gave Ekaterina the heart earring Tai Babilonia once gave her.

Kristi Yamaguchi skated many duets with Scott Hamilton during Stars on Ice shows.

One year later, the Stars on Ice skaters performed a televised tribute to Sergei entitled, "A Celebration of a Life." Scott Hamilton and Yamaguchi skated a duet on the show.

Yamaguchi was glad when the Stars on Ice organization joined forces with the Make-A-Wish Foundation®. During the tour, certain sick children were selected to watch practice sessions and have dinner with the skaters. Friendships were formed between the children and the performers, who often gave skating lessons.

The skating world was shocked when Sergei Grinkov died of a sudden heart attack in 1995. He was only 28 years old.

Spending time with these children changed Yamaguchi in a meaningful way. She wanted to do more for sick, disabled, and disadvantaged youngsters. It would take time, help, and a lot of money. But she would find a way.

Scott Hamilton

At age two Scott Hamilton developed a strange illness that stopped his growth. Years later, when Scott began skating, his illness disappeared and he started growing again. Doctors believed his recovery came from the exercise he received from skating daily in a cold rink.

In March 1981 Hamilton won the first of four World Figure Skating Championships. In 1984 he captured Olympic gold at the Games in Sarajevo and took first place at the World Championships in Canada. He turned professional that year, and has since performed in the Ice Capades, Scott Hamilton's American Tour, and Stars on Ice, a touring company he helped create in 1986. He was also its co-producer until his retirement in April 2001.

Osaka was one of the cities Kristi visited when she traveled to Japan in 1994.

Chapter 5:
Giving Back

In 1994 Yamaguchi traveled to Japan. She had been there before, but only to perform. Now she had a chance to tour the country and meet her relatives and fans. Yamaguchi visited Osaka, where she visited the Osaka City Sports Center and spent time with disabled children. She traveled to Kyoto and Tokyo, and saw her mother's family in Wakayama. It was a wonderful trip, allowing Yamaguchi a chance to understand and learn more about her Asian heritage.

Meeting An Old Friend

Performing on the Stars on Ice tour let Yamaguchi meet many people and travel to different places. In 1995 the show stopped in Vancouver, Canada. Yamaguchi and her friends attended a party to celebrate the opening of a new ice hockey arena. She saw Bret Hedican, the hockey player from the Olympics. They began to date.

Kristi first met professional hockey player Bret Hedican at the 1992 Winter Olympics.

While touring Yamaguchi continued working with disadvantaged children. She knew that even one person could make a difference in someone's life through a simple kindness or a few helpful words. But through her work with the Make-A-Wish-Foundation®, she saw that charitable organizations can reach more people than most individuals can alone.

The Always Dream Foundation

In 1996 Yamaguchi started Kristi Yamaguchi's Always Dream Foundation. Its aim is to help children through fund-raising events, held mostly in California, Nevada, and Hawaii. Yamaguchi's Foundation also supports organizations that help children, offering goods and services through its "Fulfilling Dreams" program.

Make-A-Wish Foundation

The Make-A-Wish Foundation® grants wishes to seriously ill children. The organization was founded after a seven-year-old boy named Chris Greicius got his lifelong wish to become a police officer. Chris's mother and others involved in the effort wanted to help more sick children and the Make-A-Wish Foundation was born. The Foundation now has 75 chapters throughout the United States and 28 chapters internationally. The Foundation has granted wishes to more than 125,000 youngsters. Many of these wishes include meeting role models, such as Yamaguchi.

Kristi works hard to entertain and help needy children. Here she is at an Always Dream Foundation event.

Yamaguchi's Foundation has bought computers for children's programs, taken underprivileged children shopping for back-to-school clothes, invited several youth groups to attend figure skating shows, and planned holiday parties for children's shelters. In April 2003 the Always Dream Foundation helped a mattress company give 300 new mattresses to over 24 children's shelters in Fremont, California, Yamaguchi's hometown.

A Friendship Weekend

In August 2003 the Foundation held Yamaguchi's Friendship Weekend in Honolulu, Hawaii, in partnership with the Hawaii Centers for Independent Living. The staff and volunteers from the Always Dream Foundation traveled to Hawaii to participate in the Youth Leadership Forum. The Forum was developed to give children with disabilities and their friends a chance to learn leadership and independent living skills through useful and enjoyable activities. There were sessions in beading, quilt making, swimming, computer technology, and skating.

In Her Own Words

The motto "Always Dream" has served as my personal inspiration for many years. It is my constant reminder to dream big, never lose sight of my goals, and strive to become a better person...

I realize that the dreams and accomplishments I have fulfilled are a result of my family's nurture and love. While I have been supported in the pursuit of my dreams, I realize that such opportunities do not exist for all children. For that reason, I felt the desire to create an organization whose sole purpose would be to inspire and embrace the hopes and dreams of children.

from the Always Dream Foundation website

The late 1990s were a busy time for Yamaguchi. She won the 1996 and 1997 World Pro Figure Skating Championships. She also became an author. In 1997 Yamaguchi and Kjarsgaard wrote *Figure Skating for Dummies*. Yamaguchi's **autobiography** written for children, *Always Dream*, was published in 1998. That same year Yamaguchi was inducted into the World Skating Hall of Fame.

Hall of Fame

In 1976 the United States Figure Skating Association (USFSA) started its Hall of Fame at its headquarters in Boston, Massachusetts. The purpose of the Hall of Fame was to honor skaters who have performed outstandingly over time. The USFSA and the Hall of Fame moved to Colorado Springs, Colorado in 1979. The building

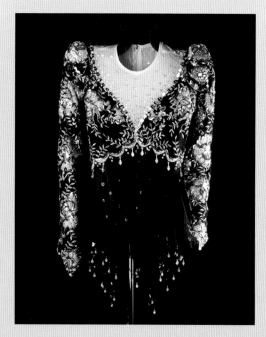

houses important skating memorabilia, including the dress worn by Kristi Yamaguchi at the 1992 Olympics.

When the International Skating Union (ISU) held its meeting at the USFSA in 1984, it was announced that the USFSA Hall of Fame would become known as the World Skating Hall of Fame, since many skating stars were from nations outside the United States.

Kristi married Bret Hedican in Hawaii on July 8, 2000.

Chapter 6:
Marriage, Motherhood, and More

Kristi and Bret Hedican became engaged to be married in 1998 in San Francisco. After three years of dating, she knew he was perfect for her. She and her family were thrilled.

The couple wanted the wedding in Hawaii. The Yamaguchis spent their vacation there every year, and Yamaguchi thought of it as another home. Hedican loved the region, too.

Yamaguchi and Hedican married on July 8, 2000. The wedding was lovely, with 300 friends and relatives and a perfect sunset over the Pacific Ocean. Yamaguchi wore a beautiful gown and a borrowed tiara. Bret wore a special vest made from a Japanese wedding **kimono**.

Few skaters have Kristi's grace, artistry, and athleticism.

Still Busy

Even while she was planning her wedding, Yamaguchi continued her fundraising and charitable work. She became more active in organizing skating benefits to support the fight against cancer. One such event, A Golden Moment: A Skating Concert on Ice, was presented in October 2000 in Oakland, California. It featured skating stars Scott Hamilton, Brian Boitano, Ekaterina Gordeeva, Kurt Browning, and several others. They performed to live music sung by famous singers such as Roberta Flack and Peabo Bryson. The show was broadcast on television the following month.

Yamaguchi also served on the Salt Lake Organizing Committee for the 2002 Olympics in Utah. She was appointed a Goodwill Ambassador during the Games, and felt proud that the United States was hosting them.

In April 2002, after 10 years with Stars on Ice, Yamaguchi decided to take a break from touring. She continued to skate on television programs, such as "Divas on Ice" in January 2003. Yamaguchi was also busier than ever with the Always Dream Foundation. The organization formed partnerships with other charities and businesses to help more people.

Yamaguchi and Hedican were eager for children of their own. In October 2003 Yamaguchi gave birth to a daughter, Keara Kiyomi Hedican. The baby was born in North Carolina, where the family lives for much of the year.

Still A Star

These days Yamaguchi enjoys grocery shopping, testing her cooking skills, and taking care of her family. Her hobbies are tennis, in-line skating, reading, dancing, photography, and watching hockey. She hopes to take piano lessons.

Yamaguchi also produces and hosts television shows, such as "Salute to American Music." And in February and March 2004, she performed at ten Stars on Ice shows, thrilling her fans.

Yamaguchi's hard work and determination in everything she does has inspired people of all ages. She has used her talent, fame, and success to help those in need, giving hope, encouragement, goods, and services. Yamaguchi's remarkable efforts have lifted her above the ranks of most sports stars. Yet to those who know her, she is still Kristi, a loyal friend, a loving daughter and sister, and a devoted wife and mother.

Kristi and Bret's daughter, Keara, was born in October 2003.

Glossary

amateur someone who does an activity for pleasure, not money

autobiography biography written by the person it is about

Axel figure skating jump requiring the skater to take off from the left front outside edge of a skate

choreographer someone who arranges dance steps and movements

endorse to publicly support a product or a person

discrimination prejudice or unjust behavior to others based on differences in age, race, or gender

federation governing group formed among states, nations, or societies

flip to turn over or perform a somersault

grant to give money or services

internment camps where people who are considered enemies are held during wartime

kimono loose, wide-sleeved Japanese robe, fastened at the waist with a wide sash

long program freestyle skating presentation lasting four minutes

loop figure skating jump in which the skater takes off and lands on the same back outside edge

Lutz figure skating jump in which the skater leaps from the back outer edge of one skate to make one full rotation in the air and lands on the back outer edge of the other skate

media means of communication with a wide reach and influence, such as radio, television, magazines, and newspapers

pairs man and a woman dancing in harmony while expressing feelings or a story through their skating

Salchow figure skating jump in which the skater leaps from the back inside edge of one skate to make one rotation in the air and lands on the back outside edge of the other skate

short program skating presentation in which the skater is required to perform three jumps, three spins, and fast step sequences in two minutes and fifty seconds

toe loop figure skating jump in which the skater takes off from the back edge of one skate, makes one full rotation in the air, and lands on the back outer edge of the same skate

triple axel jump requiring the skater to spin in the air three-and-one-half times between takeoff and landing

tribute performance or event in honor of a person

triple jump move in which the skater spins three times in the air between takeoff and landing

Timeline

1971 Kristi Tsuya Yamaguchi is born on July 12, 1971 in California.

1975 Yamaguchi sees her first ice show at a mall in California.

1980 Yamaguchi begins training with coach Christy Kjarsgaard.

1983 Yamaguchi begins pairs skating with Rudy Galindo.

1989 Yamaguchi receives a gold medal in pairs and singles events.

1989 Yamaguchi graduates from high school and moves to Canada.

1992 Yamaguchi wins Olympic gold medal in Albertville, France.

1993 Yamaguchi joins Stars on Ice tour.

1996 Always Dream Foundation is founded.

1996 Yamaguchi wins World Pro Figure Skating Championship.

1997 Yamaguchi wins World Pro Figure Skating Championship.

1997 The how-to book, *Figure Skating for Dummies* is published.

1998 Yamaguchi's autobiography, *Always Dream*, is published.

1998 Yamaguchi inducted into the World Skating Hall of Fame.

2000 Yamaguchi marries professional hockey player Bret Hedican.

2002 Yamaguchi serves as Goodwill Ambassador for the Winter Olympics in Utah.

2003 Keara Kiyomi Hedican, daughter of Kristi Yamaguchi and Bret Hedican, is born.

Further Information

Further Reading

United States Olympic Committee (eds.). *Basic Guide to Figure Skating.*
  Marquette, Mich.: USOC, 2002.

Wellman, Sam. *Female Figure Skating Legends: Kristi Yamaguchi.*
  Philadelphia, Pa.: Chelsea House Publishers, 2001.

Yamaguchi, Kristi. *Always Dream.* Lanham, Md.: Taylor Trade Publishing,
  1998.

Addresses

**Kristi Yamaguchi's Always
Dream Foundation**
1212 Preservation Parkway
Oakland, California 94612

**U.S. Figure Skating Association,
World Figure Skating Museum,
and World Skating Hall of Fame**
20 First Street
Colorado Springs, Colorado 80906

U.S. Olympic Education Center
One Meyland Hall
Northern Michigan University
1401 Presque Isle Avenue
Marquette, Michigan 49855

Index